Measuring Size

by Henry Pluckrose

Gareth Stevens Publishing
A WORLD ALMANAC EDUCATION GROUP COMPANY

Please visit our web site at: **www.garethstevens.com**
For a free color catalog describing Gareth Stevens' list of high-quality books
and multimedia programs, call 1-800-542-2595 (USA) or 1-800-461-9120 (Canada).
Gareth Stevens Publishing's Fax: (414) 332-3567.

Library of Congress Cataloging-in-Publication Data

Pluckrose, Henry Arthur.
    [What size is it?]
    Measuring size / by Henry Pluckrose. — North American ed.
       p. cm. — (Let's explore)
    Includes bibliographical references and index.
    ISBN 0-8368-2962-X (lib. bdg.)
    1. Mensuration—Juvenile literature. 2. Size judgment—Juvenile literature.
  [1. Size. 2. Measurement.] I. Title.
  QA465.P58   2001
  530.8—dc21   2001031115

This North American edition published in 2001 by
Gareth Stevens Publishing
A World Almanac Education Group Company
330 West Olive Street, Suite 100
Milwaukee, WI 53212 USA

This U.S. edition © 2001 by Gareth Stevens, Inc. Original edition © 1999 by Franklin Watts.
First published as *What Size Is It?* in the series *Let's Explore* in 1999 by Franklin Watts,
96 Leonard Street, London, EC2A 4XD, United Kingdom. Additional end matter © 2001
by Gareth Stevens, Inc.

Series editor: Louise John
Series designer: Jason Anscomb
Series consultant: Peter Patilla
Gareth Stevens editor: Monica Rausch
Gareth Stevens designer: Katherine A. Kroll

Picture credits: Steve Shott Photography cover and title page, pp. 4, 6, 11, 12/13, 19, 21,
23, 25, 27, 28, 30/31; Image Bank p. 9 (Bob Elsdale); The Stock Market p. 20 (Tom Van Sant);
Bubbles p. 15 (Frans Rombout); © C. Boretz/The Image Works p. 16.

With thanks to our models: Ashton Burns, Megan Eedle, Hattie Hundertmark, Thaddeus
Jeffries, Wilf Kimberley, and Alice Snedden.

Printed in the United States of America

1 2 3 4 5 6 7 8 9 05 04 03 02 01

Contents

We measure objects to find out their size. We can use many different words to describe an object's size, including *big, small, long, short, narrow*, or *wide*. Can you think of any other words to describe an object's size?

These boxes are different sizes. The red box is bigger than the green box. The blue box is smaller than the green box. Is the yellow box bigger or smaller than the green box?

We can measure the size of an object by comparing it to another object. This mouse is much smaller than the elephant. How big are you compared to an elephant?

These pencils are different lengths. Which pencil is the longest? Which pencil is the shortest? Which pencils are the same length?

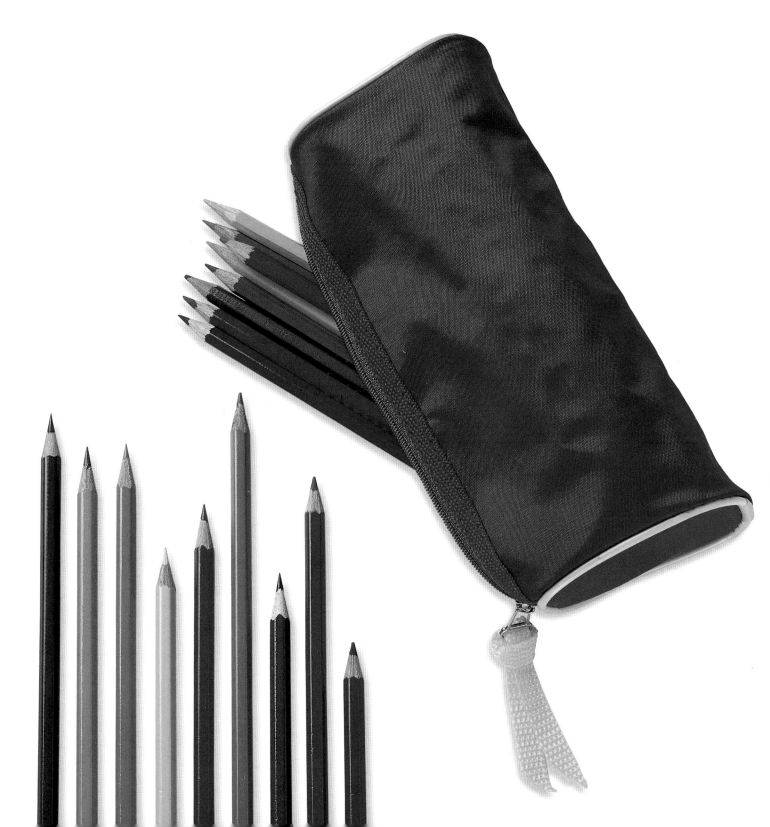

We use a ruler to measure length.
This ruler is marked in both inches
and centimeters.

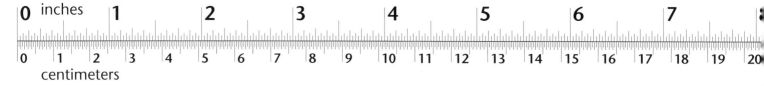

Every inch is the same length, and every centimeter is the same length. How long is this caterpillar in inches?

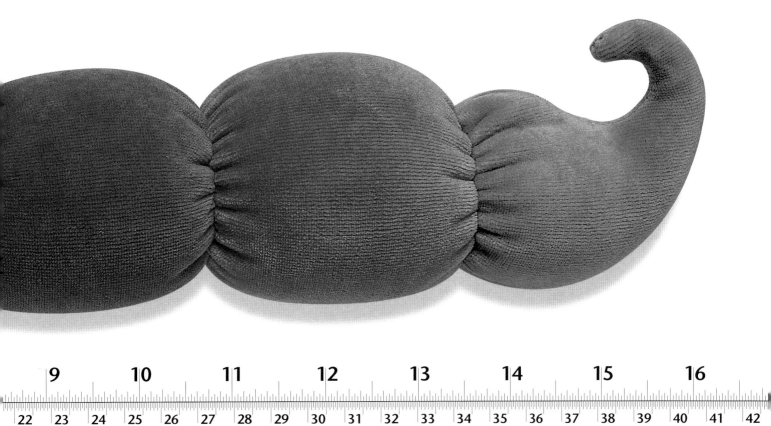

To find out how tall Karen is, Karen's mother measures her height. She measures from the bottom of Karen's feet to the top of Karen's head. How tall are you?

12 inches = 1 foot
100 centimeters = 1 meter

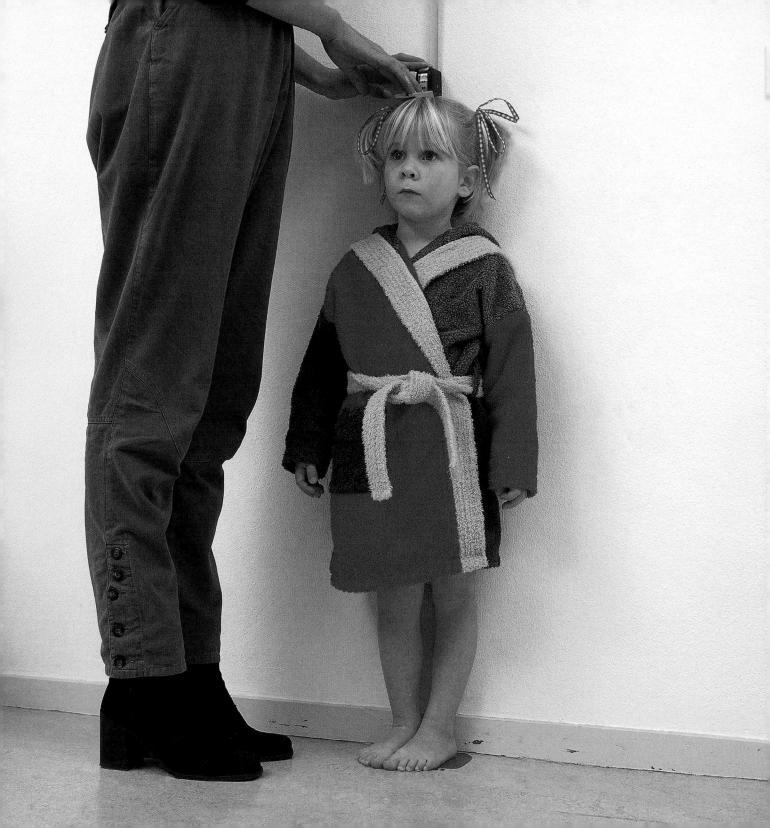

We can measure the weight of an object. We sometimes weigh letters before we mail them. Each letter is very light, but lots of letters in a mail bag make the bag very heavy.

Every object has weight. Heavy objects are measured in pounds or kilograms. This scale can measure the weight of a person. How much do you weigh?

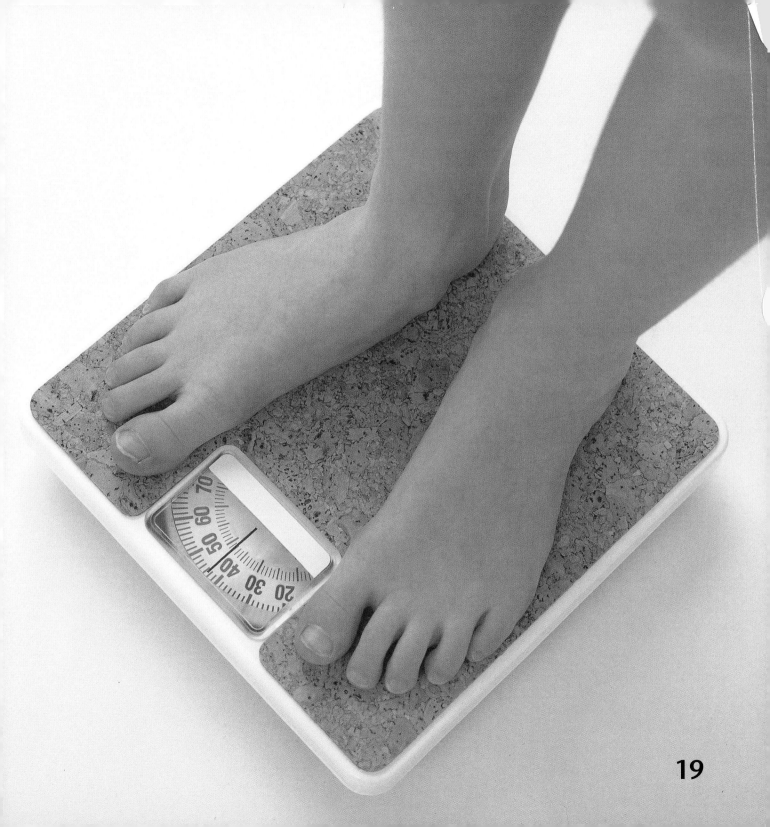

19

This ball and the balloon Katherine is holding are almost the same size. Do you think they are the same weight?

We measure water and other liquids in ounces and gallons or in milliliters and liters. These two bottles are filled with colored water. The bottles have different shapes, but they are holding the same amount of water.

23

Heidi's bucket can hold 3 gallons (11 liters) of water. The amount of liquid or the number of objects a container can hold is called its capacity. Even when a bucket is empty, it has the same capacity.

25

Jonathan is measuring 1 cup (140 grams) of flour to put into a bowl. The capacity of the bowl is 3 cups (420 g). How much more flour does Jonathan need to fill the bowl?

Monica is going on vacation. Do you think her suitcase will hold everything she wants to bring? What will Monica have to leave behind?

We can measure objects in many different ways. We can, for example, measure the capacity of this truck.

We can measure the truck's length, height, and weight, too. How many ways can people be measured?

Index

More Books to Read

The Best Bug Parade. MathStart: Comparing Sizes (series).
   Stuart J. Murphy (HarperCollins Children's Books)
Carrie Measures Up. Math Matters (series).
   Linda Williams Aber (Kane Press)
Size. Mortimer's Math (series).
   Karen Bryant-Mole (Gareth Stevens)